German South West Africa: The History and Legacy of Germany's Biggest African Colony

By Charles River Editors

The flag of German South West Africa

About Charles River Editors

Charles River Editors is a boutique digital publishing company, specializing in bringing history back to life with educational and engaging books on a wide range of topics. Keep up to date with our new and free offerings with this 5 second sign up on our weekly mailing list, and visit Our Kindle Author Page to see other recently published Kindle titles.

We make these books for you and always want to know our readers' opinions, so we encourage you to leave reviews and look forward to publishing new and exciting titles each week.

Introduction

A picture of an East African Askari soldier holding the German Empire's colonial flag

"The great questions of the day will not be settled by means of speeches and majority decisions but by iron and blood." – Otto von Bismarck

The modern history of Africa was, until very recently, written on behalf of the indigenous races by the white man, who had forcefully entered the continent during a particularly hubristic and dynamic phase of European history. In 1884, Prince Otto von Bismarck, the German chancellor, brought the plenipotentiaries of all major powers of Europe together, to deal with Africa's colonization in such a manner as to avoid provocation of war. This event, known as the Berlin Conference of 1884-1885, galvanized a phenomenon that came to be known as the Scramble for Africa. The conference established two fundamental rules for European seizure of Africa. The first of these was that no recognition of annexation would granted without evidence of a practical occupation, and the second, that a practical occupation would be deemed unlawful without a formal appeal for protection made on behalf of a territory by its leader, a plea that must be committed to paper in the form of a legal treaty.

This began a rush, spearheaded mainly by European commercial interests in the form of Chartered Companies, to penetrate the African interior and woo its leadership with guns, trinkets and alcohol, and having thus obtained their marks or seals upon spurious treaties, begin establishing boundaries of future European African colonies. The ease with which this was achieved was due to the fact that, at that point, traditional African leadership was disunited, and the people had just staggered back from centuries of concussion inflicted by the slave trade. Thus, to usurp authority, to intimidate an already broken society, and to play one leader against the other was a diplomatic task so childishly simple, the matter was wrapped up, for the most part, in less than a decade.

The German role in this complicated drama was something of an enigma. The German Empire would prove to be the most short-lived of all, for, along with the Russian and Ottoman Empires, it did not survive World War I. In 1919, Germany lost all of its African colonies, which then accrued as League of Nations mandated territories either to France or Britain. The mandate over German South West Africa, the future Namibia, was placed under British control by proxy, and its day-to-day administration was handled from South Africa. Ultimately, South Africa absorbed South West Africa as a virtual province and resisted pressure to cede authority to the United Nations for decades. Furthermore, the contest between Germany and Britain on the African continent during the late 19th century would also create the conditions that led to the North African Campaign in World War II.

German South West Africa: The History and Legacy of Germany's Biggest African Colony chronicles the politics and conflicts that marked Germany's efforts to colonize German South West Africa. Along with pictures depicting important people, places, and events, you will learn about German South West Africa like never before.

German South West Africa: The History and Legacy of Germany's Biggest African Colony

About Charles River Editors

Introduction

Scrambling for Africa

"First the merchant, then the soldier." - Bismarck

During the 16th century, the Dutch remained a strong European trading power, and the Cape of Good Hope remained a Dutch outpost, but the strategic position of the southern peninsula of Africa became more important than ever before as global trade began to develop and the British established colonies throughout the New World. The British made use of the port facilities of the Cape, but thanks to the Napoleonic Wars and the alliance between France and the Batavian Republic, it became increasingly important to British foreign policy that the Cape be secured as a British possession, against any possibility that the French might seek to claim it for themselves.

By the end of the 18th century, the Cape Colony of South Africa was a British colony, seized in 1795 from the Dutch as part of the dispensations of the fighting against the French. As a private concern, the Dutch East India Company had avoided any administrative responsibility for frontier settlements, and the Boer were left largely to their own devices.

The Boer, a Dutch colloquial term for farmer, were the descendants of the original Dutch East India Company settlers who founded the Cape Colony in 1652 as a victualling station for passing Dutch mercantile ships. The colony was established strictly for this purpose, and as a consequence, free immigration was discouraged, as was any unregulated movement beyond the confines of the settlement of Cape Town. Inevitably, however, independent immigration did take place, and this was mainly in response to the effects of the Counter-Reformation and the Catholic resurgence in Europe. The persecution of Dutch and Huguenot Protestants drove waves of both groups to search for sanctuary, and this they found at the Cape, the furthest corner of the known world.

In time, Dutch and French-speaking immigration to the Cape established the bedrock of a unique and hybridized European culture that came to be known as Cape Dutch, or *Afrikaans*. The urban settlers who settled the immediate hinterland of the Cape were, in general, highly cultured, and the metropolitan aspects of Cape Town today continue to bear this out. However, a more free-ranging and nomadic branch of the same family, driven by a far more orthodox style of Calvinism, spread out into the hinterland, evolving eventually into a rugged and independent breed of frontier pastoralists. These were the Boer, highly xenophobic in outlook and passionately independent in lifestyle. Over generations, they grew accustomed to a style of life that was itinerant, uninhibited, and unregulated. Where they encountered native Africans, they fought them, developing all the while a doctrine of entitlement not dissimilar to the biblical concept of a "promised land."

Throughout this time, the outer boundary of white settlement remained largely undefined, and beyond that, almost nothing was known about the interior. Under British rule, however, things changed radically. As a colony, the British authorities were interested in bringing the entire population, black and white, under an administrative remit, which did not sit well at all with the bucolic and individualistic Boer. The sudden introduction of British taxes, census, and land audits all irritated them unbearably, and in short order, a difficult and antagonistic relationship existed between British and Boer that continued for about three decades until the British imposed abolition. When the British forced the manumission of all slaves, it was the last straw. A series of Boer councils were held throughout the Eastern Cape, and as a result, a significant portion of the rural Boer population made the simple and fateful decision to leave.

From about 1836 onwards, therefore, a series of organized treks culminated in one of the greatest organized exoduses in modern history. About 5,000 disgruntled Boer left the Cape, and in one of the great epics of 19th century journeys through Africa, they penetrated the interior, founding two independent republics, the South African Republic, or the Transvaal, and the Orange Free State. An attempt was made to found a third republic, the Natalia Republic, on the east coast of Natal, but the British got there first, realizing that, like the Cape, Natal held too great a strategic value to be allowed to fall into unreliable hands.

A Boer family in the 1880s

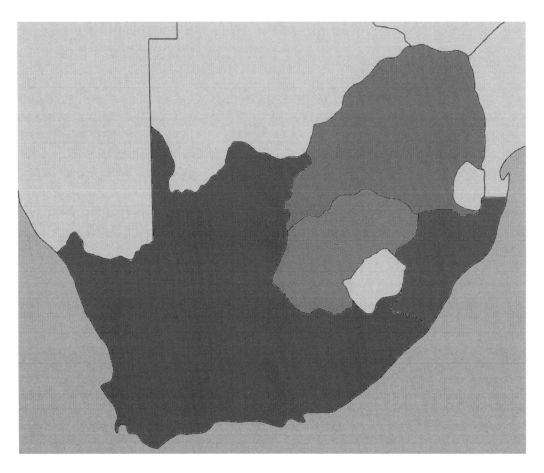

A map of the British Cape Colony (blue), Transvaal (green), the Orange Free State (orange), and the Natal (red)

This status quo might have held, but two key events took place. The first of these was the discovery of rich diamond deposits in a vaguely demarcated border region between the Cape and the Orange Free State, which inevitably altered the British view of things. That discovery was followed soon after by the discovery of what were then the richest gold fields in the world, located in the heartland of the Transvaal. Almost overnight, South Africa became the most important theater of British capital adventure in the world, and perhaps not surprisingly, the British suddenly took a keener interest in the area.

As the 1880s began, the map of Africa was undergoing a rapid evolution. Both the British and the French were beginning to occupy and claim pockets of West Africa, while the decline of the powerful Zanzibari Sultanate left a political vacuum in East Africa, which the British and the Germans hoped to fill amidst a mood of mutual suspicion.

There is a tendency today to believe that German international imperialism did not exist at all prior to the country's unification, but this is not all true. While German commercial outreach was not on quite the same scale as the British, Dutch, or Portuguese, German international business networks were nonetheless established in many parts of the world. Unlike the British East India

Company or the Hudson's Bay Company, there was little if any German ambition to officially colonize overseas regions, but 279 German consular outposts were maintained around the world, in particular in Latin America. The Hanseatic League was perhaps the earliest of German trade networks, established centuries before Germany's unification.[1] In the 16th century, the influential German Welser banking family sought to establish a territorial foothold in South America by negotiating colonial rights with Spain over an enormous enclave overlapping modern Venezuela and Columbia. The territory was known as *Klein-Venedig*, or "Little Venice," so named for the powerful Venetian trade position straddling east and west. In the end, however, it proved to be a brutal colonial experience, costing the lives of many hundreds of Germans. It was also, incidentally, the market for the importation of some 4,000 African slaves.

Thus, while the various German states traded widely in the expanding world, the commercial imperative always remained at the fore. In much the same way, the first German commercial footprints in Africa followed the expansion of Portuguese trade, and then Dutch and British trade. The first was the Brandenburg based *Brandenburgisch-Africanische Compagnie*, which, in 1682, established two trading settlements on the Gold Coast of what is modern-day Ghana. These were insubstantial efforts, however, and they did not survive. For a long time thereafter, the Germans were not active in Africa.

A particular sector of the international community that worked by default to open German spheres of influence in Africa were the missionaries. Rarely was any imperialist to be found in Africa in advance of a missionary, and like the legendary Dr. David Livingstone, missionaries often doubled as accidental explorers. Indeed, in 1848, it was the German missionary Johannes Rebmann who was the first to report to the Geographic Society of Berlin the existence of glacier-capped mountains on the African equator. Missionaries also introduced denominations and taught their version of the gospel in their own language, which inevitably became the language of local commerce and education, and before long the *lingua franca* of a region. Their chronicles and journals helped to familiarize the general public with new lands, and as international missionary outreach reached its peak during the late 19th century, the concept of colonialism more easily embedded itself in the national consciousness.

The first half of the 19th century had been the era of African exploration, with people like Livingstone and Henry Morton Stanley becoming household names, and many others dominating the various national headlines. Geographic societies flourished all over Europe during this energetic period, which in turn tended to generate a more acute appreciation of a growing middle class in the history and affairs of the world. Geographic exploration inevitably began to assume a nationalistic complexion, with nations lionizing their explorers as national heroes and claiming by default a right of involvement in any major event or discovery. In the words of German historian Winfried Baumgart, "Germany, by this time, had undergone profound economic and social changes. Between 1870 and 1900, the population of the Reich had grown from forty-one

---

[1] The *Hanseatic League* was a confederation of merchant guilds and market towns originating in north Germany in the late 1100s.

to fifty-six million. Coal production had increased from thirty-four million to 149 million tons, and steel production from 0.3 million tons to 6.7 million tons. Germany had pioneered a host of new industries and had become the chief manufacturing country in Europe. The old Prussian simplicity – lovingly described by writers such as Theodor Fontane – had widely given way to a new spirit of national self-assertion."[2]

Prior to German unification, which was completed with the return of Alsace-Lorraine at the conclusion of the 1871 Franco-Prussian War, Germany existed as a loose confederation of 38 independent states, none of which was in a position to compete in global imperialism with the likes of France or England. With the advent of the German Empire, however, things very quickly began to change. Kaiser Wilhelm I, the avuncular and old emperor of Germany, ruled through the aggressive and ambitious Chancellor Otto von Bismarck.

During his first decade in power, from about 1874-1884, Bismarck was extremely skeptical about the overall project of European imperialism, and in particular the advisability of Germany's involvement. He tended to see the German position in Europe as a more important priority than any unnecessary overseas adventures. As late as 1881, Bismarck, declared, "For as long as I remain Chancellor we will not become involved in colonialism." [3]

Ultimately, however, thanks to pressure from both within and without, he was forced to change his mind. One of the few historians to give serious treatment to this subject is Professor Sebastian Conrad of the Berlin Free University, who wrote in *German Colonialism: A Short History*, "Powerful pressure groups as well as reckless colonial pioneers in Africa forced Bismarck, to some extent against his will, into government support for the occupation of the first colonial territories in 1884."[4]

---

[2] Baumgart, Winfried, *Germans in the Tropics: Essays in German Colonial History, German Imperialism in Historic Perspective* (Greenwood Press, New York, 1987) p151

[3] Quoted from Heinrich von Poschinger (ed.), *Fürst Bismarck und die Parlamentarier,* vol. III: 1879–1890, Breslau (Trewendt) 1896, 54.

[4] Conrad, Sebastian. *German Colonialism: A Short History* (Cambridge University Press. Kindle Edition.) p1

Bismarck

For nearly 140 years, historians have wondered why and when Bismarck changed his mind. Some suggest that he was trying to pick a fight with the British, hoping to frustrate what he perceived would be the liberal, Anglophone policies of Friedrich III, heir to Wilhelm I and next in line for the throne. Others theorize that he was trying to find a way of settling matters with France in some sort of combined colonial policy which might foster a community of interest. Both seem unlikely - in all probability, he was simply responding to the mood of the times, a sense of nationalist resurgence and the power implied by empire. The last few decades of the 19th century saw public opinion in Germany shift very much in the direction of Germany claiming a more assertive role in Europe and entering more vigorously upon the "New Imperial" movement.

Another rather subtle emphasis at the time, in tandem with a resurgence of nationalism and a belief in the "Greater Germany," was the question of immigration itself. This was the age of mass emigration from Germany, mostly to the United States, and the sense was that this movement represented a net loss of German cultural integrity into the melting pot of America. Thus, the creation of colonies comprising sovereign German soil might act as a receptacle for German emigration without any loss of German national identity.

Finally, Bismarck could hardly have been deaf to the demands of capital and industry for new markets and fresh sources of raw materials. In other words, Bismarck found himself confronting a situation whereby plunging into the European drive for an overseas empire was something that the German Empire could hardly afford not to do.

On the morning of Saturday, November 15, 1884, plenipotentiaries of all of the major powers of Europe gathered at Bismarck's official residence. As each entered the yard, they were met at their carriage door by the Chancellor himself and then ushered into the library, where an informal reception took place. Then, as a body, they climbed the wide, ceremonial staircase to a second-floor reception room, where each took his allocated seat at a semi-circular table arranged before a large and detailed map of Africa pinned to the wall. Bismarck addressed the assembled delegates, outlining briefly the objectives of the meeting, after which, casting his eyes from left to right, he declared the Berlin Conference formally in session.

A depiction of Bismarck at the Berlin Conference

The Berlin Conference of 1884-85, a dry and rather formal affair, was nonetheless one of the most important and far-reaching gatherings of international power to take place at any time during the 19th century, and one that would deeply impact the course of European and African history up to the present day. In its simplest terms, the Berlin Conference sought to regulate the subdivision of Africa between the principal European powers in a manner that would not cause a major war between them. Only a somewhat desultory European interest had been shown in Africa to date, amounting to little more than a patchwork of competing spheres of influence. These were mostly private concerns — chartered companies displaying a national flag — but here and there, territories were being annexed and occupied, and in general, a rather unhealthy mood of competition was incubating over the question of Africa.

Perhaps the best example of this was the Witwatersrand, the gold-bearing region of the Transvaal Republic, nominally a British sphere of influence and certainly the most important theatre of British capital adventure of the age. South Africa at that point was divided into four separate territories - two British colonies (Natal and Cape) and two independent Boer republics (Transvaal and Orange Free State) - and between these there existed enormous suspicion and antipathy. The superior weight of British capital and imperial reach allowed the British to dominate the Transvaal gold fields, but they did so very much to the chagrin of the Boer. The Boer were not by any means impoverished because of this, but as they prospered, they were ever vigilant toward any British threat against their sovereignty.

Creating German South West Africa

"No civilization other than that which is Christian, is worth seeking or possessing." – Bismarck

When the Portuguese pressed south along the Atlantic coast of Africa and established trade settlements in many places, they abruptly came upon a vast coastal desert that persisted for over 1,000 miles until they finally passed the mouth of the Orange River. Their interest in slaves as a trade commodity was not helped anywhere along this coast, which meant there were seemingly no profits to be made by establishing any permanent settlements.

That said, one of the first Dutch explorers to leave an imprint in the sand of South West Africa was Diogo Cão, who paused briefly on the Skeleton Coast in 1485 and raised a limestone cross. The next was the legendary Bartolomeu Dias, who stopped in the region in 1487 while heading south to round the Cape of Storms.

A picture of an inscription left by Diogo Cão

After the Portuguese continued round the Cape, they established their first permanent settlement south of Angola in what would become Mozambique. In the process, they neglected to permanently settle not only the coast of South West Africa but the Cape itself, which would prove to be a cause of many regrets. Instead, it was the Dutch who settled the Cape and established the first permanent European presence in South West Africa, occupying Walvis Bay as one of few viable ports along the southern Atlantic coast. They did not, however, make any effort to push the boundaries of their settlement beyond the perimeter of the port, since the interior appeared to be nothing but dunes and gravel plains. When the Dutch lost the Cape in the late 18th century, the British assumed control over Walvis Bay, but there was still no expansion attempted beyond its original precincts.

As the Europeans increased their presence, it was not long before missionaries began appearing on the scene. The British were the first, extending their activities north from the Cape where the London Missionary Society (LMS) had been active for decades. It was under the aegis of the LMS that the first Germans of the Rhenish Mission Society were established, and it was these Germans, beginning in the 1840s, who started probing inland from the coast, evangelizing among the *Nama* and *Herero* people. Missionary work was confined to the southern fringes of the desert, and success was minimal, simply because the inhabitants were ephemeral, few in numbers, and scattered over a vast region. The population was mainly *San* and *Nama*, and they displayed little interest in Christianity, education, and the other hallmarks of what the Europeans considered the bounties of "civilization." As a result, the work, at least in the beginning, was thankless and unproductive.

Then, in 1883, a year before the Berlin Conference convened, an itinerate German trader by the name of Adolf Lüderitz purchased from the local *Nama* chieftainship the district of *Angra Pequena*, marked and so named in 1487 by Bartolomeu Dias. He renamed the area "Lüderitz" after himself.

Lüderitz

Lüderitz, a romantic and hopelessly quixotic adventurer, was an itinerant privateer and trader, born in Bremen in 1834, who wandered overseas in search of wealth and opportunity. He was not particularly successful in any of his destinations until he wandered south towards the Cape from the Lagos Colony, called in on the coast of South West Africa, and there observed a country unclaimed by any European power. The reason it was unclaimed was due simply to the fact there was little besides empty desert beyond the port, and there were few inhabitants, but nonetheless, Lüderitz was intrigued. He and his companion Heinrich Vogelsang, a fellow Bremen merchant, devised a bold and impractical scheme to found a colony. His stated objective in his application for German protection was to provide an alternative to America for the droves of German immigrants leaving the Fatherland, and no doubt this was at least part of it. The quest for adventure was another, and the possibility of making money was likely the most critical of all.

Though it aimed to be a destination for mass migration, the coast of South West Africa did not offer much promise, but Lüderitz did at least enjoy an excellent natural port and a small population of native people with whom to trade. Missionaries arrived soon afterwards, and around a small port, a reasonably prosperous town grew. Besides British-held Walvis Bay, several hundred miles to the north, Lüderitz was isolated by hundreds of miles of desert.

Lüderitz himself grew reasonably affluent, but nothing offered the fabulous wealth that the mineral magnates of South Africa enjoyed. As it turned out, however, his timing was superb, because it was precisely around this time that Bismarck was beginning to warm up to the inevitability of a German overseas empire, and if there was anywhere that he wished to pitch his tent, it was in the middle of a British jamboree. The discovery of diamonds in South Africa, the rumors of gold nearby, and the growing tensions between the British and the Boer all combined to recommend the official establishment and naming of a German colony in South West Africa.

The region of interest to the Germans was broadly defined at the time as "Damaraland," and the geographic delimitation of Damaraland as it is understood today is the interior region of the top third of modern Namibia. The country as a whole is arid, blending from true desert in the south and center to dry woodland in the north. It is a land of striking landscapes and natural artistry, with a rich natural history, but a thinly scattered human population eking out a scant survival on a hostile landscape. The earliest residents were the *Khoisan* peoples and their closely related cousins, the *Damara*. While the origins of this branch of *Khoisan* society is obscure, it is certainly linked to similar and interrelated people of Khoisan roots scattered across the region, from the central highlands of Angola to the Cape Peninsula. As is typical of a nomadic, hunter-gatherer lifestyle, both groups were widely dispersed, tending to the maintenance and administration of small family and kinship groups. This meant the people were politically weak and militarily insignificant.

Another branch of the *Khoisan*, known as the *Nama*, appeared in the southern precincts of Namibia in or around the 1st century BCE, introducing for the first time a cattle-based pastoral society. To the north, in the regions that border southern Angola, where a slightly higher rainfall regime offered increasingly improved pasture and hunting grounds, the population was larger. There, ancient societies of *San* mingling with increasing intensity with new arrivals, the people of the Bantu language, probed southwards from the tropical forest of the Congo Basin.

This was part of a much greater social permutation known as the "Bantu Migration" or the "Great Bantu Expansion." The Bantu Migration remains more of an evolving and contested theory than a provable historical process, but by whatever means it took place, and whatever might have been its stimulus, commencing at about 1000 BCE, an expansion began of Bantu-speaking people from the region of the Niger Delta. Over the centuries, the Bantu filtered south and east, populating the tropical center and channeling south along the avenue of the Great Rift Valley. Eventually, this movement reached the plains and savannas of southern Africa, and after the people crossed the central highlands of Angola, they arrived on the edges of the northern Kalahari (in what would today be southern Angola), the Caprivi Strip, and Ovamboland (in northern Namibia). These were ancestors of the *Ovambo* and *Kavango*.

Another Bantu-speaking group that penetrated somewhat deeper into the interior of the country and thus made more substantial contact with white colonists was the *Herero*, perhaps the most famous Namibian ethnic group. They were a nomadic, pastoral people, roaming the desert savanna with their herds of sheep, goats and cattle. They reached the region as part of a particular wave of inbound migration that originated in the central African lakes region, entering from the northwest of modern Namibia. As they continued to move southwards, entering Damaraland, a group remained behind in the *Kaokoveld* region, emerging in due course as the *Himba* people.

All of this ensured by that the start of the 19th century, the future territory of German South West Africa had no major tribal confederations or any substantial indigenous societies, so there would be no means of organized resistance to deal with the inevitable intrusion of European influence. In the beginning, however, that influence tended to be indirect. The first Europeans to make permanent landfall on the southern subcontinent of Africa were the Dutch, who arrived in 1652 to establish a victualling station for passing ships of the Dutch East India Company. From this emerged the Boer, and while they encountered some resistance from the *San* and *Nama* people, the latter at least also adapted white lifestyles, language, dress and weaponry, eventually taking on the name *Oorlams*.

The *Oorlams*, incrementally displaced from their traditional ranges, crossed the Orange River with their herds of cattle and began aggressively monopolizing the best grazing land. At the same time, the *Herero* were pushing south, also occupying tracts of viable grazing land on the fringes of the desert. All of this served to disturb for the first time the tranquility of primordial life that had endured for millennia.

In the wake of the *Oorlams*, there came a group known as *Basters*, the *Besters,* or the *Bastards*. As the name implies, the *Basters* were a group derived from sexual relationships among the original Cape Dutch and their racial intolerance. They belonged to a wider demographic known then, as they are today, as "Coloured," the product of generations of miscegenation. However, because of their mixed blood, they were generally unwelcomed in both black and white society. They were, however, Afrikaans-speaking, Calvinist Christian, and more inclined to identify with their white cultural lineage than their native. They settled in what would be central Namibia, establishing their capital in the town of Rehoboth. There, they would briefly attempt to establish a style of independent republic, the "Free Republic of Rehoboth," adopting a constitution and a system of elected government which survived only until the arrival of the Germans.

By then, European missionaries were already beginning to filter into the country, which, thanks to the *Oorlams* and the *Basters*, was already predominantly Christian. Agents of the London Missionary Society, active in the Northern Cape, founded the town of Bethanie in the south of the territory, building what is believed to be the oldest church in Namibia. On the back of the

LMS came the German Rhenish Mission Society, initially the smaller of the two, but destined soon to enjoy the advantage of a sympathetic government. In each case, however, Christian influence was minimal in the wider countryside, which remained uncontacted by *Oorlam*, *Baster* or European missionaries.

It was into the midst of this that Adolf Lüderitz arrived and established his trading station on the coast, founding the first organized settlement flying the German flag. In 1884, still acting somewhat on his own initiative, Lüderitz placed his settlement under formal German protection in the hope of discouraging the British, who held the enclave of Walvis Bay, from extending their interest any further south. In fact, the British were rather inactive during this period, as the premiership rotated between Prime Minister William Gladstone and Benjamin Disraeli, the former a liberal and the latter a fiscal conservative. This ensured the Germans had no real concern about a preemptive British takeover, at least for the time being. There certainly were cautionary voices in the Cape, not least among them the British capital imperialist Cecil John Rhodes, warning that the Germans were poised to seize the entire southwest coast of Africa, but the risk of this seemed not to register with the British government back in London at the time.

Rhodes

The danger that Rhodes and others envisioned was that a German colony in the southern region would directly compromise British control, not only of the Cape but also of the newly discovered diamond and gold reserves that transformed the economy of the entire region. Another point that Rhodes was apt to make was that the complete void of cooperation between the British and Boer in South Africa, which was already degenerating slowly to a state of inevitable war, offered the opportunity for the Germans to strike an alliance with the Boer that held the very real potential of pushing the British out of the Cape and Natal.

Rhodes was certainly right about all of this, but the British government did not initially move to forestall a German protectorate in South West Africa, and they would soon come to regret the inaction. On August 7, 1884, two months before the doors opened on the Berlin Conference, the German flag was formally hoisted at Lüderitz, and a protectorate was declared over German South West Africa. Thus, the deed was done, and this occupation, along with others all across

Africa, would be ratified at the Berlin Conference, after which the colony of German South West Africa formally came into being. The process was simple and straightforward, brokered 5,000 miles away in Europe and achieved without a drop of blood being shed. For the most part, it made absolutely no difference to the people of the hinterland, whose lives, at least for another few years, remained undisturbed.

The next question to be answered was that of the natural hinterland, and perhaps more importantly, what was to comprise the economic backbone of the colony. Lüderitz, for all that he was owed by the German public, was never conspicuously successful, and the port fees and trade with a widely dispersed and primitive population held very limited prospects. Commercial cattle production might possibly be viable in the north and in pockets of the interior, but on the surface, there seemed very little in the way of economic potential to justify any inward expansion.

Then came the discovery of diamonds, followed by gold, copper, and platinum, and almost overnight German South West Africa had an economy. In 1885, the *Deutsche Kolonialgesellschaft für Südwest-Afrika*, or the "German Colonial Society for Southwest Africa," was floated, backed by various banks, industrialists, and politicians, and then granted blanket rights to develop and exploit the mineral wealth of the new colony. The assets of Lüderitz's failing enterprise were bought out, and German South West Africa fell under de facto private economic control. This operated much the same way Cecil Rhodes' British South Africa Company and Sir George Goldie's Royal Niger Company assumed early responsibility of colonizing, pacifying, administering and exploiting their respective regions – Rhodesia and Nigeria – under the blanket authority of a Royal Charter.

Thereafter, Bismarck guided the legislation creating the new colony based on the proposition that the colony would be self-supporting, developed and exploited by private capital, and privately administered under the broad aegis of a colonial governor, or commissioner. The first colonial commissioner appointed was the explorer Gustav Nachtigal, who was a somewhat obvious choice insofar as he was the German government's plenipotentiary at large in Africa. He served as consul-general to Tunisia, and then as commissioner-general for German West Africa, and in German South West Africa he served as something of a placeholder for the more substantial appointment in 1886 of Heinrich Ernst Göring. Heinrich Göring, the father of the Nazi Luftwaffe commander Herman Göring, tended to set the tone for the subsequent colonial administration.

Nachtigal

Heinrich Göring

There is very little detailed information available about the inclusion of natives in the German administration in the colony, largely because it did not develop a comprehensive system and indigenous people were marginalized either by economic coercion or brute force. The likes of the *Basters* and the *Oorlams* were absorbed with little resistance, maintaining a certain exclusivity of culture, but blending reasonably easily into Protestant German society, albeit with stringent social limitations. Of the native peoples, the *San* were not dealt with in any particular way, but the *Nama*, allies of the *San*, began their resistance almost immediately, led by the legendary Hendrik Witbooi, their dynastic leader.

Witbooi

The British might have attempted to combine force with management as they did in other places across Africa, but Göring's response was to simply try to exterminate the adversaries. As such, military operations against the *Nama* were typically heavy-handed and merciless. It certainly helped that the *Nama* were also at war with the *Herero*. As for the *Herero*, Göring negotiated a treaty of protection, which was signed by both Göring and Kamaherero, the *Herero*'s paramount chief, in October 1885, ostensibly in response to a plea by the *Herero* for German protection.

In the meantime, European settlement in the region gathered momentum through the 1890s and towards the turn of the century. Immigrants were attracted by the boom in mining, the urban trades, and the availability of land. From the south, Afrikaans-speaking immigrants moved northwards incrementally, as did miners and mining engineers, while the urban and professional classes tended to derive from Germany. Reflecting both the official position and the attitude of white South Africans moving north, relations between the races were tense, acrimonious, and uncooperative. In other colonies across southern Africa, like Rhodesia and Nyasaland, the interactions between settlers and natives were less rancorous at first, as the benefits of modern medicine, law and order, education and the cash economy eased the transition. None of these benefits were ever extended in any meaningful way to the natives of German South West Africa, where the indigenous groups held onto their traditional lifestyles with tenacity, mostly rejecting Christian outreach and resisting efforts to draw them into a formal labor market.

Given all of that, and the manner in which the Germans were going about administering the colony, a significant incident seemed inevitable.

Kamerun and Togo

"From little date seeds, great things are born." – Namibian Proverb

While German South West Africa and German East Africa were the two flagship territories of the German African Empire, the two colonies of Togo and Kamerun were also briefly annexed by Germany.

Cameroon today is a largely French-speaking country, with a significant English-speaking population associated with neighboring Nigeria. It is situated in the armpit of the Gulf of Guinea, and its German colonial origins are now rather obscure. As with most other West African regions, the colonial complexion of the coast was defined by early trade settlements, followed by the arrival of missionaries, and in due course annexation against the overall backdrop of the Scramble for Africa. The first German factory to be established on the coast of Kamerun was near the capital of Douala in 1868, rather late in the trade rush in West Africa considering it began with the Portuguese in the late 15th century. Various German trading concerns contributed investment and development, and a plantation economy quickly usurped orthodox trade with the native people, which tended to be the pattern elsewhere.

That said, the typical principle of chartered companies prevailed here as it did elsewhere, and perhaps the most influential private capitalist to invest in agriculture and mixed trade in Kamerun was Adolph Woermann. Woermann was a German merchant, shipowner and politician with deep and varied interests in West Africa, and it was he, allied with Lüderitz to the south, who lobbied the German government to formalize the annexation of the various German "spheres of influence." By the 1880s, significant German investment had been injected into the region, mainly in the form of large agricultural concerns and plantations on land theoretically purchased from local chiefs.

Woermann

There was never any particular drive to colonize the territory, but vaguely Bismarck mulled over the idea of linking German Kamerun through the Congo with German East Africa, which was then beginning to fall in increments under German control. The French were similarly trying to push their influence through the region of the Upper Congo and the Ubangi rivers to gain access to the Upper Nile, as a means of linking their expanding territories with French Somaliland. The Germans, however, were minor players in this region, and Bismarck was soon enough disabused of any such grand, continental-scale maneuvers. German claims over Kamerun in the end abutted against the French occupation of Chad, and it was there, in time, that the boundary between the two powers was established.

Meanwhile, despite the lack of German immigration, the colony was developed with characteristic German precision and thoroughness. Comprehensive rail, road, and postal networks were established for the purposes of facilitating agricultural production and effective administration, and at no time does there appear to have been any particular problems for German business interests posed by the native people. Afro-European trade was by then very well established, and highly sophisticated indigenous institutions cooperated easily with the Germans to the broad benefit of both sides. The lack of European settlement was mainly due to an incompatible climate, which in turn meant that disputes over land and resources were absent, as was discontent over labor and taxation. Before those kinds of issues could inevitably rise up, Kamerun would pass out of German hands as a consequence of Germany's defeat in World War I, after which the colony tended to look to its mandated powers, France and Britain, for cultural and political direction. To this day, German is not spoken anywhere on mainland West Africa.

Central to the story of Kamerun was Gustav Nachtigal, an imperialist who found himself leading the various lobbies to petition the German government to extend protection over the colonies of West and South West Africa. He also served at various times as commissioner and commissioner-general of all. By the standard of the time, German interest in West Africa, both economically and territorially, was minimal, and in the end it would be France that would accrue the lion's share. Nachtigal, in the meanwhile, headquartered on the Spanish island of Fernando Po, actively coordinated the legal and political process of establishing both the colony of Kamerun and Togoland.

Togoland did not enter the German family of African dependencies quite as easily and willingly as Kamerun. By the time the Germans had developed their momentum in terms of colonization, most of Africa north of the equator was in one way or another under the influence of Britain or France. Togoland, which is today the nation-state of Togo, was taken by the Germans through the forcible signing of treaties of protection with local chiefs, forming the basis of the German claim when the matter was reviewed as part of the Berlin Conference. Togoland, as viewed on a contemporary map, amounts to a narrow sliver of territory squeezed between the British Gold Coast (the future Ghana) and French Dahomey (the future Benin). It was then, as it remains today, an anomalous and dissociated territory, a product of boardroom map-drawing with little relevance on the ground in terms of traditional boundaries and tribal delimitations.

As with other places in West Africa, the German footprint was rather light, and under tropical conditions the attraction of the territory for German settlement was minimal. Its existence was strategic insofar as Germany desired above all to be a player on the European imperial scene, and Togoland was probably as quintessential a prestige colony as any European claim in West Africa. In 1890, for example, a grand total of 12 ethnic German officials managed an administration ruling over millions, even as the expatriate European population rarely if ever exceeded 1,000.

Despite the lack of Europeans, the territory was developed with a view to expanding plantation agriculture, with cacao, coffee and cotton dominating production. Again, the colony was dominated by private capital and buttressed by one of the first German colonial constabularies, the *Polizeitruppe*, which was involved in ongoing operations against rebellious tribes and chieftainships. Indeed, resistance against German rule was ongoing, and in the first decade of the 20th century, some 35 military-style operations were conducted to suppress local rebellions. Through it all, Togoland proved uniquely successful, at least economically, and Lomé, the capital of the colony, enjoyed a reputation as the most scenic and pleasant of all the European ports emerging on the Atlantic coast of Africa.

The success story would be brief in duration, as the results of World War I led to the colony being granted to the French as a mandated territory. It continues to count itself as a member of the Francophone bloc of West African territories.

The Scramble in Southern Africa

"I repeat that superior races have a right, because they have a duty. They have the duty to civilize inferior races." – Jules Ferry

An important aspect of the Scramble for Africa was the momentary ambition of the German imperial parliament to extend German control across central Africa from German South West Africa to German East Africa. In the immediate aftermath of the Berlin Conference, along with those territories being mopped up in West Africa, a significant swath of central Africa remained unclaimed by any European power. This region runs congruent with the modern states of Botswana, Zimbabwe, Zambia and Malawi, and its strategic value to all of the major colonizing powers, with the exception of France, was enormous.

The Portuguese were established on the coats of modern Mozambique and Angola, and thanks to ancient trade traffic between the two, they imagined themselves the primary claimants to all of the territory in between. There was some justification for this, as Portuguese slave traders and military adventurers had indeed for centuries plied the route of the Zambezi Valley and hunted the plateaus on either side for slaves. However, Portugal was very much in decline during the late 19th century, and its claims tended to be limited by its ability in the moment to finance formal administration and occupation.

The British, on the other hand, led by Cecil John Rhodes, saw the same region as vital in the pursuit of the Cape to Cairo objective which was increasingly becoming the blueprint of British activity continent-wide. At the same time, the Germans looked across the great divide and saw the potential to link up their colony of German South West Africa with German East Africa, throwing an effective girdle across the middle of the continent. This would not only frustrate Portuguese ambitions but would bring an immediate halt to the vaunted British ideal of linking the Cape to Cairo.

The Portuguese introduced into the Berlin Conference what they styled the "Rose-Colored Map," a rather fanciful depiction of Africa with its central regions painted in the Portuguese *rosé*. Naturally, this gained absolutely no international recognition, and the race was narrowed down to German and British, both potentially heirs to the future of central Africa. British consul Henry O'Neill, based on Mozambique Island, dismissively noted, "To speak of Portuguese colonies in East Africa is to speak of a mere fiction—a fiction colourably sustained by a few scattered seaboard settlements, beyond whose narrow littoral and local limits colonisation and government have no existence."

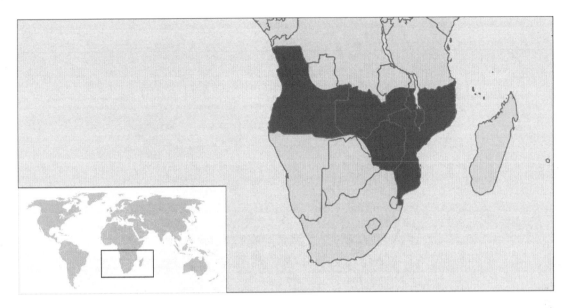

The Rose-Colored Map

The contest between the Germans and British would be set in Bechuanaland, a vast and amorphous tract of desert and semi-desert to the north of South Africa and east of German South West Africa. It was congruent, more or less, with modern-day Botswana, and in the mid-1880s it was effectively unclaimed and unsettled by any European power. The region did, however, witness periodic efforts by the Boer of the Transvaal to establish satellite republics and colonies, which occasionally unsettled the British. The primary British agent of imperialism in South Africa at the time was still Rhodes, and he lobbied a reluctant British government relentlessly to declare Bechuanaland a British protectorate, which it resolutely refused to do.

At the same time, German and British agents were jostling and maneuvering in the court of the *amaNdebele* King Lobengula. The kingdom of the *amaNdebele*, a powerful, centralized monarchy of great military prowess, comprised the southern two-thirds of what would in the future be Zimbabwe, which was seen as the gateway to future Zambia and Malawi, all of which was as vital to one party as the other.

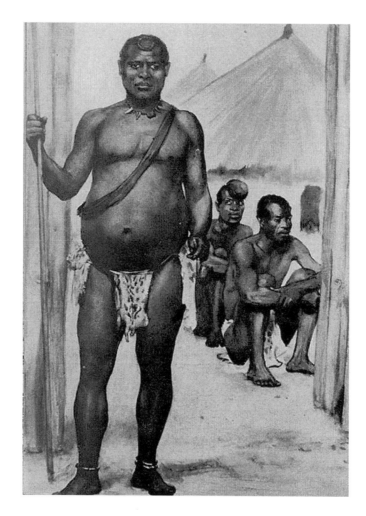

A sketch of Lobengula

As the Germans established their South West Africa colony and Rhodes engineered the Bechuanaland Protectorate, things in Lobengula's neighborhood began to change most profoundly. Suddenly, he was no longer dealing with the occasional prospector or missionary, but a concentrated European effort to pin him down to a treaty of protection, or indeed any treaty that might be construed as such. The capital of *kwaBulawayo* (the Place of Slaughter) was besieged by concession seekers representing private and public interests from across the European colonial spectrum. Each was working against the interests of the others, and among them was plenty of intrigue, backstabbing, lies, and deception. All that Lobengula knew for certain was that if he succumbed to the urging of his commanders (his *indunas*) to wipe the entire gaggle out with a single order, a foreign army would be on his borders in months, if not weeks.

It was into this situation that an old Boer hunter from the Transvaal Republic by the name of Piet Grobler, a fluent isiNdebele speaker and a cordial acquaintance of Lobengula, appeared. The exact circumstances of what happened are unknown, but somehow Grobler was able to secure Lobengula's signature on a vaguely worded treaty of amity and friendship with the Transvaal.

The potential of this treaty was that it might give the Transvaal Republic the right to annex Matabeleland as an extension of the republic, with the further possibility that the Germans would piggyback on this to put their foot through the door, and thus gain an option.

As it so happened, however, on his way back to the Transvaal from Matabeleland, Grobler disappeared, along with his treaty. It has never been established precisely what became of him, and conspiracy theories have since abounded, but in all likelihood he fell victim to bandits and his treaty was somehow lost. The very existence of it, however, set the pot boiling, and when news of it reached Rhodes, it shocked him into immediate action.

When news of the Grobler Treaty reached Rhodes, he realized that that time to act was now. All things considered, he was in a very strong position, but it was imperative that he gain some sort of similar treaty from Lobengula to offset any potential claim from the Transvaal, and to give himself some time and space to maneuver.

His first course of action was to approach the British High Commissioner to the Cape, Sir Hercules Robinson, in an attempt to browbeat him into arbitrarily declaring a British protectorate over Matabeleland, which he was empowered to do. At this time, however, Robinson would not do so under just his own authority. He instead echoed Rhodes' own instincts to get something on paper – anything at all – just to buy time.

Robinson

Rhodes then approached a 53-year-old ex-missionary by the name of John Moffat, then part of the Bechuanaland colonial administration, and requested that he travel on Rhodes' behalf to

Bulawayo to negotiate a treaty with Lobengula. Moffat was an excellent choice, because, as an ex-missionary, he knew Lobengula well. His father, the famous Scottish missionary Robert Moffat, enjoyed the rare benefit of a friendship with Mzilikazi, and their two sons grew up in association with one another. Moffat, as a liberal and a humanitarian, understood that implicit in Rhodes' advances would be the end of the amaNdebele nation, but as much as he might have respected the amaNdebele as a race (as most whites did) the nature of the regime was abhorrent to him, and Moffat believed it would in the long term be to the benefit of both the amaNdebele and the maShona to come under British protection.

Moffat, with surprising ease, was able to persuade Lobengula to attach his seal to a document. This treaty, apart from a vague promise of cooperation and friendship between the British and his independent people, bound Lobengula to enter into no "correspondence or treaty with any foreign state or power to sell, alienate or cede or permit or countenance any sale, alienation or cession of the whole or any part of the said amaNdebele country under his chieftainship, or upon any other subject without the previous knowledge and sanction of Her Majesty's High Commissioner for South Africa."

The terms of the Moffat Treaty, however, were not specific enough to frame an application for a royal charter, so a second delegation was assembled on behalf of Rhodes' British South Africa Company to negotiate something more absolute. For this mission, Rhodes chose a business partner by the name of Charles Dunell Rudd, a tall and austere man in his mid-40s who was practical and severe. Accompanying him was a lawyer, Rochford Maguire, and an interpreter and "native expert" by the name of Francis Thomson. Also assisting was an Anglican missionary by the name of Charles Helm, who was fluent in isiNdebele and somewhat trusted by Lobengula.

Rudd

The Rudd Concession, as it came to be known, forms the bedrock of modern Zimbabwean history. For the forces of colonization, it was celebrated as a feat of frontier diplomacy, and the basis upon which the territory was occupied. From the point of view of black liberation history, however, it was a massive deception and the quintessential act of political duplicity that set the tone for the colonial era to follow.

Either way, Lobengula remained in a desperate quandary. By 1889, when Rudd and his group first appeared in Bulawayo, the frenzy of foreign petitions had reached a fever pitch. The competition was now intense, and at the hands of a few key players, Rudd among them, Lobengula found himself under unrelenting pressure. Adding to that was even greater pressure from below to order a military solution, which of course he knew that he could not do. Lobengula teetered on the brink of a nervous breakdown.

In the end, after months of prevarication, and endless sessions in consultation with different people, Lobengula came to the decision that he had no choice but to deal with the most powerful of his enemies. Bearing in mind the strength of the British in southern Africa and the apparent authority of Rhodes, who Lobengula understood to represent the British imperial establishment, he was eventually persuaded to sign the document that Rudd held in front of him. He could not have known that Rhodes did not actually represent the British imperial authorities, but merely his own interests in the form of the British South Africa Company. Rudd, naturally, did not disabuse Lobengula of this belief, so when he affixed his seal to the Rudd Concession, it was the native leader's belief that he was dealing with Queen Victoria.

The Rudd Concession as Lobengula negotiated it and understood it contained several key points. Most importantly, entry into Matabeleland would be restricted to 10 miners who would claim no land and who would remain subject to amaNdebele law. No specific territorial grants or concessions were made, and no permission for general settlement was granted. In exchange, a generous cash payment was offered, along with a quantity of guns and ammunition.

When the terms appeared in writing, however, the implications were very different, and since Lobengula was illiterate, he relied on Reverend Charles Helm primarily to interpret and sign off on the fact that everything was as it should be. Helm, however, lied to him by claiming the treaty was as it had been negotiated, when in fact it was not. The implication of the document was that the British South Africa Company was empowered to exploit as it pleased every mineral resource in Matabeleland, and by extension Mashonaland, and to take whatever measures were necessary to achieve this, with no mention whatsoever of any fealty to amaNdebele law or government.

Believing what he was told, Lobengula affixed his seal to the document, and before the ink was dry, Rudd was on horseback hurrying back to Kimberly to hand the document over to Rhodes. With equal haste, Rhodes then boarded a ship and made his way to England to submit an application for a royal charter.

Naturally, as news began to circulate, there were plenty of other people ready to alert Lobengula to the fact that he had been duped. He had no idea at all what he had done, but he sensed that whatever it was, it was not good. Moreover, no one would give him a straight answer because they were all trying to scupper Rhodes' victory and obtain one of their own at the 11th hour.

It was one thing to engineer a spurious legal entry into Matabeleland, but it was another thing to actually physically seize it. Lobengula and his army may not be capable of deflecting the might of the British Empire, but they certainly retained the potential to fight. Eventually, the British would manage to settle the territory, and their efforts put a check on any German ambitions to expand out of South West Africa.

All of this coincided with the establishment and advance of German East Africa, pushing southwards from the equator as aggressively as the Germans pushed from the north, and the front line of the Anglo-German contest soon enough shifted north to the region of the great lakes and the central plains.

Somewhat against expectations, South West Africa did indeed prove to be a viable colony for German settlement. The cool southern Atlantic Ocean mitigated the worst conditions of the interior, and under the almost temperate conditions of the coast, settlements were founded and towns were established. The economy centered on trade, fishing and mining, and, across vast tracts of savanna, ranching.

It was the ranchers' demand for land that ultimately triggered the *Herero* and *Nama* uprisings. The story of the genocide of the *Herero* and *Nama* people of Namibia was one of the darkest stains of European imperialism, and it had massive implications.

European imperial regimes varied from the light touch of intellectual liberalism in the Cape to the rule of the shackle, the bullet, and the *knout* that characterized Belgium King Leopold's Free Congo. The British generally maintained elitist but balanced and lawful colonies, while the Portuguese combined haphazard administration with complete indifference to social boundaries. The French blended *liberté, égalité, fraternité* into their general imperial policy, making them at times the most liberal and egalitarian of colonizers. There were certainly individual German administrators and military commanders who added their philosophical contribution to the civilizing mission of empire, but in general, when push came to shove, the Germans were quick to resort to the iron fist.

Across their imperial spectrum, the Germans dealt with a number of high-profile native rebellions, and in each case, the response was violent and disproportionate. Nowhere was this truer than in their dealings with the *Herero* and the *Nama*.

The pressure on land began with the *Oorlams* and gathered pace with the arrival of the *Baster*, who, in both cases, maneuvered and contested for control of the best grazing lands. Neither the *Herero* nor the *Nama* was armed to any extent, and certainly not organized for sustained war. They were, as a consequence, very easily marginalized, and as Europeans began to occupy the land, in particular around the turn of the century, indigenous herdsmen were either pushed out into the desert fringes or forced into labor. It has been commonly reported that the *Herero* were forced into slavery, which does not appear to have been the case, at least not in any systematic manner. In fact, the sad truth is that if they had submitted more willingly to labor, they might perhaps have suffered a less disastrous fate. There is also considerable debate over the term "genocide" when describing the German response, but there is plenty of documentation and anecdotal evidence to suggest that extermination as a policy was at least discussed.

Be that as it may, the issues remained the alienation of land and expulsion of native herdsmen. The process seems to have been rather arbitrary, and while there was some discussion of demarcating native reserves, reflecting the British native administrations of Kenya, Nyasaland and the two Rhodesias, the policy was never adopted.

While one can scour sociological journals to theorize on the nature of race relations in colonized Africa, which varied significantly from place to place, and between the various powers, on a purely anecdotal level there is no doubt that a dark undercurrent of unusually severe racism characterized society in South West Africa. The Germans' sense of racial superiority was no doubt one contributing factor, and the original aspects of a native society of nomadic habits and primitive technology led Europeans to turn up their noses at the indigenous populations, but mostly it was a question of competition for viable land in desert country.

It was the *Nama* who rose first in rebellion, led by their charismatic leader Hendrik Witbooi. Between 1892 and 1894, a low-level guerrilla war was fought, until, in 1895, the *Nama* were driven to an unconditional surrender. Under the terms of that surrender, *Nama* fighting units were required to fight under German command against the *Herero*, their traditional enemies, and in various other minor campaigns to suppress smaller groups.

In response to this, the *Herero* leadership began to organize, planning a revolt in hopes of returning to some utopian state of the past. The leader of the movement was Kamaharero, the paramount chief of the *Herero*. The orders given by Kamaharero on the eve of rebellion reveal an interesting selectivity: all whites were to be slaughtered, with the exception of missionaries, English and Boer. *Basters* and other "coloured" peoples would also be spared. This implies that it was the Germans specifically that the *Herero* wished to destroy and remove, and perhaps also that English and Dutch speaking colonists were not necessarily aligned with the Germans, at least not morally.

This order of a general slaughter has since come under dispute, with a majority of historians now tending to believe that the revolt was spontaneous and that written orders were circulated only once it began. Either way, on January 12, 1904, a small, mounted force of *Herero* invaded the cattle ranching town of Okahandja in central South West Africa, murdering 123 whites, almost all German.

In most of Africa at that time, with the possible exception of South Africa, white communities were at all times vastly outnumbered by native people, and always at risk of annihilation at the hands of a discontented native population. The principle of European inviolability was based on the perceived superiority of the European race, and the whites relied on a heavy and usually disproportionate response to any hint of trouble. It was for this reason, as much as anything, that the Germans responded to organized rebellions with the weight that they did.

The rebellion, once it began, spread quickly, and before long, due to reasons still not well understood, Hendrick Witbooi and the *Nama* war parties joined forces with the rebellious *Herero*. Thereafter, while the *Herero* were the greater in numbers, most of the organized fighting was done by mounted commandoes of *Nama* riflemen. The *Nama*, indeed, were by then masters of guerrilla warfare, familiar with the landscape, fluent in survival, and free to move around an almost unlimited battlefield.

The Germans responded by rushing in a significant expeditionary force, which subsequently employed a strategy of capture, containment, and scorched earth. The hero of the campaign, at least as far as the Germans were concerned, was Lieutenant-General Lothar von Trotha, one of the most notorious people in the history of African imperialism. He was appointed commandant of forces in South West Africa on May 3, 1904 with specific orders to crush the *Herero* rebellion. He arrived in the colony in June 1904, and within two months the elusive rebels were run to ground and pushed to fight in the decisive Battle of Waterberg on August 11, 1904.[5] The Germans surrounded the rebels with a force of 1,625 mounted infantry, supported by a battery of field artillery and 14 machine guns. A force of some 5,000 rebels, along with their families, were given the bleak option of surrendering or departing east into the vast reaches of the Kalahari Desert. While the *Herero* opted to fight, the battle was brief and one-sided, and it ended with a disorganized retreat as the rebels were driven into the desert, continually harassed and shot on sight whenever encountered or captured.

---

[5] The Waterberg Plateau of Namibia lies in the north-central region of the country.

Trotha

It was this forlorn episode that accounted for most of the deaths associated with the genocide of the *Herero*, due in large part to mass starvation, but also because of the notorious practice of poisoning wells. Concentration and labor camps also contributed to many deaths, and in the end, over 60,000 *Nama* and *Herero* lost their lives, about 70% of the population.

Trotha was hardly circumspect about the extermination. One of his ultimatums read, "I, the great general of the German soldiers, send this letter to the Hereros. The Hereros are German subjects no longer. They have killed, stolen, cut off the ears and other parts of the body of wounded soldiers, and now are too cowardly to want to fight any longer. I announce to the people that whoever hands me one of the chiefs shall receive 1,000 marks, and 5,000 marks for

Samuel Maherero. The Herero nation must now leave the country. If it refuses, I shall compel it to do so with the 'long tube' (cannon). Any Herero found inside the German frontier, with or without a gun or cattle, will be executed. I shall spare neither women nor children. I shall give the order to drive them away and fire on them. Such are my words to the Herero people."

Another order of his read, "This proclamation is to read to the troops at roll-call, with the addition that the unit that catches a captain will also receive the appropriate reward, and that the shooting at women and children is to be understood as shooting above their heads, so as to force them to run [away]. I assume absolutely that this proclamation will result in taking no more male prisoners, but will not degenerate into atrocities against women and children. The latter will run away if one shoots at them a couple of times. The troops will remain conscious of the good reputation of the German soldier."

There have been attempts by sympathetic writers and historians to suggest that Trotha was not conscious of the likely implications of his orders when they were made, and that he did not have genocidal intentions. There may be some truth in this, but there was certainly a movement in the colony to be rid of a people who would not easily bend to formal labor and who at least theoretically were competing for the vital resource of land. Moreover, it hardly seems possible, that a formal and heavily enforced policy of exile into the desert would not result inevitably in a large number of deaths. In the natural course of events, had the tribes been left *in situ,* some sort of a settlement would be necessary which would involve the concession of some amount of land to them, and this was not a popular solution for a majority of colonists.

While Trotha emerged from this episode as a national hero, there inevitably hung about his name an aura of ill repute that could never quite be expelled. The policy of extermination was only exposed and stopped by the relentless work of local missionary organizations, although they too emerged from the chapter with reputations deeply tarnished. The missionaries were seconded to persuade the surviving *Herero* to surrender and enter containment camps. By then, the survivors were in a wretched condition, and many did. From large, centralized containment camps, they were distributed to small camps around the country as de facto prisoners of war. One modern historian explained, "Herero prisoners of war were used as labor by both military and civilian enterprises for a wide range of activities. Prisoners were put to work in civilian companies, ranging from laundries to transport contractors, breweries and shipping companies. Various military units used their prisoners, often children, primarily for the maintenance and care of their stock. This entailed the construction of cattle kraals, the pumping of water, and the cutting of grass for fodder and herding. The German colonial civil administration used its Herero, and later Nama prisoners of war, for the building of railway lines between Usakos and Otavi, and later between Lüderitz and Keetmanshoop."[6]

Undeterred, Trotha insisted in the aftermath, "It was and is my policy to use force with

[6] Quoted: Gewald, Jan-Bart. *Colonization, genocide and resurgence: The Herero of Namibia 1890-1933*, 2000, p206-207

terrorism and even brutality." In fact, he would cite his treatment of the *Herero* as a warning to the *Nama*: "The Nama who chooses not to surrender and lets himself be seen in German territory will be shot, until all are exterminated. Those who, at the start of the rebellion, committed murder against whites or have commanded that whites be murdered have, by law, forfeited their lives. As for the few not defeated, it will fare with them as it fared with the Herero, who in their blindness also believed that they could make war successfully on the powerful German Emperor and the great German people. I ask you, where are the Herero today?"

The ensuing carnage ended with about 10,000 *Nama* killed and another 9,000 detained in camps.

War in South West Africa

"I am not a man who believes that we Germans bled and conquered thirty years ago [to be] pushed aside when great international decisions are made. If that were to happen, the place of Germany as a world power would be gone forever. I am not prepared to let that happen." – Kaiser Wilhelm II

On April 12, 1877, two years before the Anglo-Zulu War, the British had actually annexed the Transvaal in a bloodless and peaceful operation led by none other than Theophilus Shepstone. From there, it was widely assumed by the British that they could bring about the submission of the Orange Free State.

As it turned out, the generally peaceful reception of British rule in the Transvaal was dangerously deceptive. A majority of the Boer remained deeply inimical to the British and any presumption of the absorption of the Transvaal into the British Empire. Popular resistance simmered for the next few years, until, on December 20, 1880, a brief war broke out. Known as the First Anglo-Boer War, it caught the British by surprise, and in the course of a few weeks, sovereignty of the Transvaal went back to the Boer.

The matter was temporarily shelved as the frenzy of the gold rush washed over the Transvaal, and its economy was radically transformed. The Transvaal was now no longer impoverished but awash with gold revenue, and it was arming itself. Nonetheless, the question of British sovereignty over all of South Africa continued to preoccupy the metropolitan political establishment, and thanks to the sudden and meteoric wealth of the region, that preoccupation steadily grew.

A large part of British anxiety over the continued independence of the Transvaal lay in the sudden proximity of the Germans. In 1885, the German Empire annexed the territory of Damaraland, which would eventually become the German colony of South West Africa and later become Namibia. By then, the leaders of the various nations believed that the different countries' global expansion would heighten tensions among the Europeans and bring about a global war.

To deal with that eventuality, the security of British strategic interests in southern Africa was vital, and the weak link in that regard was the Boer.

The British and everyone else understood that the Boer's hatred would possibly lead them to ally with Britain's enemies. There was also something of a natural ideological alliance between the Boer and the Germans, so there was every reason to suppose that a political and security alliance would soon follow. It is questionable how much better an alliance with Germany would be compared to an alliance with Britain, but that certainly appeared to be the direction that things were going, and if that happened, it could position the Germans to take over the entirety of South Africa and its goldfields, diamond fields, and strategic ports. This was something the British could obviously not tolerate, and if the Boer could not be induced to peacefully accept British sovereignty, they would have to do so under force of arms.

The Transvaal Boer, led by an aging patriarch named President Paul Kruger, resolutely resisted calls by various expatriate lobbies (the Boer referred to the non-Boer émigré community as Uitlanders, or Foreigners) to provide limits on taxation, and representation commensurate with that taxation. The Uitlander population, by the latter half of the 19th century, had grown in numbers and capital influence to such a degree that a free grant of voting rights would have meant, in practical terms, an Uitlander government in the Transvaal. Gone in an instant would be the cherished Boer ideal of independence, sovereignty, and freedom from British domination. Kruger could simply not countenance this.

Kruger

Sometime during 1895, Rhodes, still based in the Cape, formed a covert alliance with the Conservative British Colonial Secretary, Joseph Chamberlain, who happened to share his vision for a united South Africa, albeit for different reasons. Rhodes was a capitalist and a visionary, and there was always a strong strain of ideology that ran through his thinking. Chamberlain, on the other hand, was a political strategist, and he was concerned with the proximity of the Germans, the potential of a German/Boer alliance, and the likely implications this had on Britain's strategic position in Africa. Chamberlain also worried about a wider European war being inevitable.

Chamberlain

While carefully camouflaging his involvement, Chamberlain tacitly supported the development of a plot in South Africa, devised by Rhodes and supported by Rhodes' local network. In essence, the plot involved leveraging Uitlander discontent in the Transvaal to create a coup d'état. Rhodes would provide the arms and the money, and he would orchestrate the start of the coup. That trigger would take the form of a mounted force of some 600 men, drawn from the colonial militia of his territory of Rhodesia. At a predetermined time, the Uitlanders in Johannesburg would rise in rebellion, and the armed force, led by a man named Leander Starr Jameson, would ride into the city, take control of the gold mines, and then engineer the collapse of the Transvaal government.

As it turned out, Rhodes made one major miscalculation, and it was simply that wealthy men are seldom predisposed to revolution. A great deal of hue and cry was generated, and a rather amateurish organization of the plot ensured that the Boers were well-informed of every detail, so that when the raid was launched on New Year's Eve of 1896, the Uitlanders manifestly declined to place themselves in harm's way and the raiders were met by a fully armed Boer reception party.

As Julius Caesar once remarked, if one must break the law, then do so to seize power, but in all other cases, obey it. Rhodes failed to seize power, so he simply broke the law. Chamberlain, the complicit British Colonial Secretary naturally distanced himself from the planning and denied all knowledge, leaving Rhodes to bear the consequences alone. The raiders were extradited to Britain to face trial, while Rhodes was eventually removed from all of his major business interests and forced to resign as Prime Minister of the Cape Colony. He never achieved the same level of power and influence again.

An 1896 depiction of the arrest of Jameson

Although it was an abject failure, the Jameson Raid set in motion a chain of events that would lead to war. The Uitlander crisis continued to ferment, and the British authorities in South Africa, supported by Whitehall, initiated negotiations with the government of the Transvaal over the question of Uitlander rights and liberties in the republic. These negotiations were somewhat disingenuous since the British were looking to instigate some sort of conflict, and in due course, as he was backed into a corner, President Kruger issued an ultimatum for the removal of British troops from the borders of the republic. The British press bellowed with derisive mirth at the audacity of it, as did the Victorian public, and the ultimatum was ignored.

Thus, on October 11, 1899, war was declared. The Second Boer War would end up being much more difficult for the British than anticipated due to the nature of the guerrilla insurgency waged by the Boer, but that would help various British military officers learn counterinsurgency tactics ahead of World War I. Just as importantly, this war involved contingents and forces from many different parts of the British Empire, making it somewhat of a precursor to a world war.

While the Germans were not directly involved in the war, indirectly they were deeply implicated. Although the German imperial authorities never formally threw their support behind the Boer, a number of Germans fought alongside the Boer as private citizens, and most Boer combatants used German manufactured Mauser rifles and Krupp artillery, all sourced and imported before the war. During the war, German arms imports were limited by a British naval blockade, and upon the British occupation of the Boer capitals, they ceased altogether.

The net result of the Boer War was a reasonably secure British victory, with the establishment soon thereafter of military rule over two new colonies. These were the Transvaal Colony and the Orange River Colony. Once united with the two older British colonies, the Cape and Natal, in 1910, the Union of South Africa was formed. A key element of this union, despite its status as a British dominion, was that it existed under local leadership, specifically under the premiership of Prime Minister Louis Botha and deputy Jan Christian Smuts. Both men were ex-commanders of the Boer fighting forces, and allies of Britain only by necessity, and by political agreement. The British, at least in part, understood that a major European war was pending, and it was inevitable that Britain would need to call on South Africa when that war broke out.

Smuts

Botha

German South West Africa, in the meanwhile, was home to the deep-water port of Walvis Bay, still a British enclave, but surrounded by German territory and vulnerable at any moment to a takeover in the case of a war. It was also the location of a German long-range communication tower, all of which presented a very real potential threat to Allied shipping in the South Atlantic during World War I.

When the Great War started in August 1914, the British realized the German territory had to be taken, but in the early stages, they found themselves neither equipped nor organized to mount any kind of operation against German South West Africa, so the responsibility fell on South Africa.

For their part, the Germans acknowledged their relative weakness in Africa in relation to their strength in Europe, so it was understood that the defense of German colonies in Africa would not be with a view to defeating the British or the French, but to lock up as much Allied resources and manpower in Africa as possible. It was generally believed that the Central Powers would emerge victorious in Europe, after which the Germans could negotiate over Africa from a position of strength.

Another major factor was the deep reluctance of South Africa to enter into a war on behalf of the British Empire just 14 years after the bitter defeat of the Boer. By then, the character of the British Empire had evolved, and the principal territories were no longer as closely allied to the center as they had once been. Increasingly, the empire was being referred to as a "Commonwealth," with each territory allied to the Crown but enjoying nominal independence. India remained under direct rule, and although a certain amount of diplomatic maneuvering was required, India's entry into the war on the Allied side was never really in doubt.[7] A vague commitment to consider dominion status in the aftermath of the war mollified the growing Indian nationalist movement, while Australia and New Zealand were increasingly part of the Asian security equation, which involved concerns about the potential of Japanese imperial ambitions, and Canada was now much more engaged with the United States in terms of trade and security.

In South Africa, the situation was far less certain. South Africa was a British dominion, but its collective loyalty to the British Crown was very much in doubt. A little over a decade earlier, one of the most bitter imperial wars on record had been fought between the two white races of South Africa, and the notion of reconciliation so soon afterward, to the extent that South Africa would willingly go to war for Britain, was untested to say the least. At the same time, the German Empire was as close to a foreign relation as the Boer republics had. Thus, while a significant number of South African servicemen did not acknowledge either the British as an ally or the Germans as an enemy, the expectation that they fight on those terms was sure to open up wounds that had barely begun to heal. Indeed, there was a strong movement among the hardline Afrikaner faction which nurtured a hope that, with the British fully preoccupied with war in Europe, an opportunity might be there to evict them from South Africa altogether and reestablish the republic.

Soon after the declaration of war, a formal request was submitted to South Africa to annex German South West Africa with its own resources. This was obviously a major request and a significant responsibility, but General Botha and General Smuts agreed without hesitation. Smuts' appreciation of the British was not without reservations, but both men recognized that if South Africa did not firmly and resolutely hitch its wagon to the British side, then it would most certainly be left behind and would never realize its full potential as a member of the first tier of global nations.

---

[7] The Indian nationalist/independence movement was fully formed by then, and agitation of Indian dominion status was well underway.

While this reality was also acknowledged by many others, it was rejected by the vast majority of Afrikaans-speaking South Africans. By then, the difficulties of race and ideology in the Union of South Africa had already manifested themselves in a series of bitter and violent labor disputes, centered on the Witwatersrand but affecting industry throughout the Union. The causes of the various strikes and lockouts were general, but underscoring this industrial action was the steady rise of Afrikaner nationalism and a determination to protect white, Afrikaans-speaking workers against unfair competition from lower-paid blacks. Much of the anger expressed was directed at the government (Smuts and Botha in particular), and as World War I began, the stability of the government and the feasibility of a British dominion hung very much in the balance. Smuts and Botha were seen by a majority of their colleagues and compatriots as having sold out to the British, and the decision of the government to honor the British request to mount a campaign against the Germans in South West Africa was seen as clear evidence of this.

Despite internal opposition, both Botha and Smuts were determined to carry it through. In part, this was to establish the principle of South African loyalty to the British Crown, but also to prove that the Union of South Africa was viable and a regional superpower. Furthermore, while a South African campaign to annex South West Africa would, in theory, add the territory to the dominions of the Crown, in practical terms, it would add territory to South Africa.

Smuts, as Minister of Defense, had the responsibility for creating the Union Defence Force, or UDF. This proved to be a delicate, political balancing act, which required fair Boer representation at a command level, but at the same time established an armed force that would be both stable and obedient to the civilian government. To command the UDF, Smuts appointed Brigadier-General Christian Beyers, the highly respected and senior Boer War commander. Beyers' loyalty, however, was first and foremost to the Afrikaner nation, and not necessarily to the government. Although he remained loyal to both Botha and Smuts as fellow members of the Afrikaner nation and as comrades in arms, he was not a supporter of the pro-British position of the government.

In fact, Beyers was bitterly opposed to South African participation in the war, and in this regard, he was backed up by some very powerful voices. The aging General Jacobus de la Rey was one of these. He stood firmly against South African participation in the war, and what he had to say about it was taken seriously in many quarters. On September 15, 1914, Beyers resigned his commission, writing, "It is sad that the war is being waged against the 'barbarism' of the Germans. We have forgiven but not forgotten all the barbarities committed in our own country during the South African War."[8]

Meanwhile, stationed in the Northern Cape, along the frontier with German South West Africa, was a force of about six-hundred 600 UDF members under the command of General Salomon

---

[8] Beyers was referring to the use of concentration camps to isolate Boer women and children from the fighting men, to starve out the latter. Thousands of Boer women and children died in these camps.

"Manie" Maritz. Maritz was a "bitter-ender," which in South African parlance meant one who advocated a fight to end rather than surrender at the end of the Boer War. In mid-September 1914, in the midst of preparations to mount the South West Africa Campaign, Maritz led his commandos across the Orange River and into South West Africa and declared for the Germans. He also declared a provisional government and announced the removal of the Union of South Africa from the British Empire.

GENERAAL MANIE MARITZ.

Maritz

Smuts had certainly been expecting something along these lines, and he seized the opportunity when it came to stamping the authority of the government on the rebellious armed forces. Martial law was declared, and the "Maritz Rebellion" was systematically crushed. A commando unit under the command of Beyers was also attacked and destroyed. With what can only be described as extreme prejudice, Smuts acted swiftly and decisively to bring the matter to a conclusion. In the end, he was able to retain the loyalty of the armed forces, which, albeit reluctantly and with deep reservations, held firmly to the policy of war on behalf of the Allied Powers.

When the dust settled, it was quietly acknowledged that the loyalty of the UDF hung on a knife's edge, and for a while South Africa teetered on the very brink of civil war. However, now that it was over, Smuts was at last in a position to plan the South West Africa Campaign, and he set about doing this immediately.

South Africa conducted two major military campaigns during the war, known as the German South West Africa Campaign and the German East Africa Campaign. The former was fought between September 1914 and July 1915, and it marked the coming of age of Smuts as a military genius, which was surprising because he had no formal military training at all. He entered service during the Boer War after the collapse of the republics, at which point the guerrilla phase of the war had already started. Prior to that, he held the position of State Attorney of the Transvaal and had never fired a shot in anger. In fact, many anecdotal reports say that he never did, conducting numerous successful operations and campaigns without ever personally resorting to gunfire. His brilliance was in tactical assault and evasion, and a wider strategic appreciation of waging war. He was awarded the rank of general in the informal manner of the Boer commandos, and he retained that rank for the remainder of his life as a mark of respect.

The German South West Africa Campaign was the first chapter of mechanized desert warfare in the annals of military history, and it remains the essential template for similar wars and campaigns. Upon analysis, however, it was more of a feat of logistics and military engineering than military maneuver, which would often be the case in desert warfare. The Germans did not defend the colony with a great deal of commitment, resting on the assumption that they would achieve victory in Europe and then get back any lost colonies elsewhere across the world. Early in the war, that was a fair position to take since the odds of a German victory were good, so the strategy in Africa was simply to tie up as much Allied manpower as possible in a wild goose chase from one end of the colony to another, offering surrender only when run to ground.

The broad strategy of the South West Africa Campaign was a vast double envelopment. Two armies were deployed, one commanded by General Botha and the other by General Smuts, landing respectively at Walvis Bay and Swakopmund and attempting to trap the defending garrison in a giant pincer. The strategy was simple enough and sound, and its success can be attributed almost entirely to the vast logistical feats of fielding an army, supplying it under punishing conditions, and providing wells and roads and railway lines upon which it could move forward. The Germans remained one step ahead until they could no longer do so, and they then surrendered in good grace. As far as World War I campaigns went, this one was remarkably bloodless, with the South Africans losing 185 killed (most in non-combatant circumstances) and the Germans just over 100. The territory was placed under a military government for the duration of the war, leaving General Smuts to turn his attention to German East Africa.

Ideally, the British wanted General Botha to command and lead the Allied forces in the German East Africa Campaign, but the war remained so deeply unpopular in South Africa, so it was decided that he would remain in South Africa and run the government. A British officer,

General Sir Horace Smith-Dorrien, was instead appointed by the War Office to take command of the East Africa Campaign, but en route to South Africa, he fell ill and was unable to take up his command. After much consideration, the job was given to Smuts.

The difficulty in this regard was that Smuts was not a member of the British Army, nor any army for that matter, and he had never undergone any sort of formal military training. This time, he would be commanding a British and Commonwealth force, so it was necessary for him to hold a British Army commission. He was therefore quietly inducted into the British Army as an honorary member with the rank Lieutenant General, which, at 47, made him the youngest man to date to be awarded that rank.

East Africa was divided between the British and German empires along the broadly speaking line of the modern frontier between Kenya and Tanzania. By international treaty, it was understood that the colonial possessions of each empire would not prosecute the war, maintaining neutrality for the sake of not exciting the natives.[9] Both colonial governors were committed to honoring this convention, but the German military attaché in East Africa, Colonel Paul Emile von Lettow-Vorbeck, had other ideas. His objective, not unlike that of the German commanders in South West Africa, was to force the commitment of as much Allied manpower as possible into a largely irrelevant theater simply to ease pressure against German forces on the Western Front. By then, the certainty of a German victory in Europe was not quite so keenly felt, and the strategy was to avoid a general defeat.

Initially, von Lettow-Vorbeck commanded the battlefield. The British territory (Kenya and Uganda) was only protected by a weak, colonial militia, a handful of imperial troops, and a few battalions of the King's African Rifles. Inevitably, with a weight of naval superiority, the British were able to blockade the coast and main ports of German East Africa, which included sinking the German warship SMS *Königsberg* in a daring operation, but they lacked the resources to dislodge the Germans from the interior in and around Mount Kilimanjaro. From that stronghold, using the local *Schutztruppe*, or native troops under German command, von-Lettow-Vorbeck conducted a campaign of attrition into British territory. He repeatedly targeted the Uganda Railway, which ran parallel to the international frontier.[10]

Smuts arrived in the theater in February 1916 at the head of a large South African force. Now energized, the British turned the tide of the campaign, after which von-Lettow-Vorbeck adopted the strategy of a fighting retreat, leading the Allied forces in a mobile operation that continued until a few weeks after the signing of the Armistice in November 1918.[11] The Allied victory, such as it was, represented another feat of logistics as von Lettow-Vorbeck, leading a largely

[9] This was the Main Act of the Berlin Conference of 1884/5

[10] The *Schutztruppe*, or colonial protection force, comprised battalions of native troops, or 'askari', commanded by metropolitan German officers. Von Lettow-Vorbeck went on a recruitment drive early in the war, and at its peak, he commanded a force of about 20,000 men at arms, with many more in auxiliary roles.

[11] The East African Campaign of WWI is regarded as the longest running campaign of WWI. It began at the moment of the declaration and ended only after the signing of the Armistice. Von Lettow-Vorbeck offered his surrender but did not acknowledge defeat.

native army, ranged across the East African interior. Troops from India, several parts of British Africa, as well as Rhodesia and South Africa were employed in the theater, along with hundreds of thousands of native carriers and porters. In the end, the East Africa Campaign degenerated into a battle more against the conditions of tropical warfare than enemy action, with several times the casualties recorded from disease than from contact with the enemy. Neither side could definitively claim victory or defeat, and in the end, von Lettow-Vorbeck and Smuts acknowledged one another's brilliance. They later became friends.

German-held Togoland was of particular strategic interest to the Allies for reasons of a powerful wireless transmitter that provided an important link in the German communications chain between Europe, Africa, the South Atlantic and South America. The campaign to deal with it was a combined Anglo-French operation, mounted from the neighboring colonies of Gold Coast (British) and Dahomey (French). Again, the Germans did not attempt a concentrated defense, but simply did what they could to complicate the inevitable. The German administration in Lomé attempted to claim neutrality under the terms of the Congo Act, but this carried no weight whatsoever. Allied forces began moving in within a few days of war being declared, and by August 6, 1914, French forces, almost entirely comprising black troops, were in occupation of Lomé, the capital of German Togoland. Thereafter, German forces, also comprising mostly black troops, fought a light rearguard action, surrendering on August 22 in the Battle of Chra. By the standards of World War I, the casualties were practically insignificant, with 83 British, 54 French, and 41 Germans killed.

The campaign to take Kamerun faced more resistance. The campaign involved forces from British Nigeria, and from the French and Belgian Congo. The operation, once again, commenced almost at the moment that war was declared, and continued in a large and sprawling theatre for over a year. The Allies, however, occupied the strategic coastal cities and ports reasonably quickly, utilizing assets of the Royal Navy, after which the Germans retreated to the mountainous interior and held off Allied attacks until the spring of 1916. Once defeat was inevitable, they sought asylum in the neutral Spanish held territory of Río Muni (Spanish Guinea).

In the cases of both German Togoland and Kamerun, an Anglo-French occupation force assumed administrative control until the end of hostilities in Europe, after which both were placed under Anglo-French mandated control as wards of the League of Nations. Britain was granted control of the hinterland of Kamerun since it abutted the borders of Nigeria, while the French took the southern quadrant as it aligned with the frontiers of Gabon and French Congo. In much the same way, British Togoland and French Togoland were created, with the French taking about 60% of the territory as it aligned with the borders of French Dahomey, and the British assumed administrative control of the region closest to the Gold Coast.

While the most famous mandates established by the League of Nations went to Britain and

France in the Middle East, it was South Africa that was given an exclusive mandate over the territory of South West Africa. This, on the surface at least, was part of the British mandate, but in reality it was a reward to South Africa for the conquest of the German territory.

Smuts regarded this as entirely just, but he was aggrieved somewhat when South Africa was not given East Africa in respect of the dominant South African role in that campaign. There was, by then, already a degree of wariness in Whitehall over the apparent micro-imperialist ambitions of South Africa, and while handing over South West Africa, 95% percent of which was desert, was one thing, East Africa was another altogether. The Tanganyika territory thus became a British mandate, which, incidentally, finally created the reality for Cecil John Rhodes' Cape to Cairo vision.[12]

The South African mandate over South West Africa would evolve into de facto South African annexation, after which successive South African governments tended to regard the territory as a fifth province of South Africa. Under the terms of its mandate, the territory remained under the control of the League of Nations, and then the United Nations, but South Africa's refusal to relinquish control of the region when requested to do so would subsequently set the tone for later confrontations between South Africa and the international community.

The dissolution of the German Empire had obvious ramifications in Europe, as the Treaty of Versailles meted out a draconian punishment that helped fuel the rise of Nazi Germany, but it also had a massive impact on Africa. With the British holding onto African colonies in the wake of World War I, the stage was set for more European adventurism on the continent. During World War II, the main prize was the Suez Canal, and the geopolitical hinterland of this region, which included not only the Mediterranean, but the Red Sea. These positions were of major strategic value for global shipping, and North Africa also held symbolic value for the Italians, who were in search of a revived Roman empire under Mussolini. For the Allies, it was the only theater of war where the fight could be taken to the enemy, making it a means to relieve pressure on Britain in the vital summer of 1940 and then on Russia when Hitler's attentions turned east in 1941.

As the Italians faltered there, the Germans would end up dedicating more resources than Hitler anticipated to North Africa, including sending the legendary Desert Fox, Erwin Rommel. As a result, a direct link could be drawn from the vanquished German Empire and its African colonies to the Third Reich and one of the most notorious campaigns of World War II.

Online Resources

Other books about African history by Charles River Editors

---

[12] The relevant British territories included South Africa, Bechuanaland, Southern Rhodesia, Northern Rhodesia, Nyasaland, Tanganyika, Kenya, Sudan, and Egypt. Each was a British dependent territory or a British protectorate.

Further Reading

Aldrich, Robert. Greater France: A History of French Overseas Expansion (1996)

Atkinson, David. "Constructing Italian Africa: Geography and Geopolitics." Italian colonialism (2005): 15–26.

Axelson, Eric. Portugal and the Scramble for Africa: 1875–1891 (Johannesburg, Witwatersrand UP, 1967)

Boddy-Evans, Alistair. "What Caused the Scramble for Africa?" African History (2012). online

Brantlinger, Patrick. "Victorians and Africans: The genealogy of the myth of the dark continent." Critical Inquiry (1985): 166–203. online

Chamberlain, Muriel Evelyn. The scramble for Africa (4th ed. Routledge, 2014) excerpt and text search

Curtin, Philip D. Disease and empire: The health of European Troops in the Conquest of Africa (Cambridge University Press, 1998)

Darwin, John. "Imperialism and the Victorians: The dynamics of territorial expansion." English Historical Review (1997) 112#447 pp: 614–642.

Finaldi, Giuseppe. Italian National Identity in the Scramble for Africa: Italy's African Wars in the Era of Nation-building, 1870–1900 (Peter Lang, 2009)

Gjersø, Jonas Fossli (2015). "The Scramble for East Africa: British Motives Reconsidered, 1884-95." Journal of Imperial and Commonwealth History. Taylor & Francis. 43 (5): 831–60. doi:10.1080/03086534.2015.1026131. Retrieved 4 March 2016.

Hammond, Richard James. Portugal and Africa, 1815–1910: a study in uneconomic imperialism (Stanford University Press, 1966)

Henderson, W. O. The German Colonial Empire, 1884–1919 (London: Frank Cass, 1993)

Hochschild, Adam (2006) [1998]. King Leopold's Ghost: A Story of Greed, Terror, and Heroism in Colonial Africa. London: Pan Books. ISBN 978-0-330-44198-8.

Klein, Martin A. Slavery and colonial rule in French West Africa (Cambridge University Press, 1998)

Lovejoy, Paul E. Transformations in slavery: a history of slavery in Africa (Cambridge University Press, 2011)

Lloyd, Trevor Owen. Empire: the history of the British Empire (2001).

Mackenzie J. M. The Partition of Africa, 1880–1900, and European Imperialism in the Nineteenth Century (London 1983).

Oliver, Roland, Sir Harry Johnston and the Scramble for Africa (1959) online

Pakenham, Thomas (1992) [1991]. The Scramble for Africa. London: Abacus. ISBN 978-0-349-10449-2.

Penrose E. F., ed. European Imperialism and the Partition of Africa (London 1975).

Perraudin, Michael, and Jürgen Zimmerer, eds. German colonialism and national identity (London: Taylor & Francis, 2010)

Robinson R,. and J. Gallagher, "The partition of Africa", in The New Cambridge Modern History vol XI, pp 593–640 (Cambridge, 1962).

Rotberg, Robert I. The Founder: Cecil Rhodes and the Pursuit of Power (1988) excerpt and text search; online

Sanderson G. N., "The European partition of Africa: Coincidence or conjuncture?" Journal of Imperial and Commonwealth History (1974) 3#1 pp 1–54.

Sparrow-Niang, J., Bath and the Nile Explorers: In commemoration of the 150th anniversary of Burton and Speke's encounter in Bath, September 1864, and their 'Nile Duel' which never happened(Bath: Bath Royal Literary & Scientific Institution, 2014)

Stoecker, Helmut. German imperialism in Africa: From the beginnings until the Second World War (Hurst & Co., 1986.)

Thomas, Antony. Rhodes: The Race for Africa (1997) excerpt and text search

Thompson, Virginia, and Richard Adloff. French West Africa (Stanford University Press, 1958)

Wesseling, H.L. and Arnold J. Pomerans. Divide and rule: The partition of Africa, 1880–1914 (Praeger, 1996.)

Free Books by Charles River Editors

We have brand new titles available for free most days of the week. To see which of our titles are currently free, click on this link.

Discounted Books by Charles River Editors

We have titles at a discount price of just 99 cents everyday. To see which of our titles are currently 99 cents, click on this link.